101 Gar[...] [...]y
Whilst Socially
Distancing

– For Children Aged 3 To 7

By

Martin Williams

Early Impact

www.earlyimpactlearning.com

CONTENTS

About The Author 1

Introduction 3

Chapter 1: Sitting In Pairs Games 10

Chapter 2: Chalk On The Floor Games 20

Chapter 3: Memory Games 30

Chapter 4: Listening Games...42

Chapter 5: Rope Or String Games..53

Chapter 6: Classic Outdoor Games (With A Twist) 60

Chapter 7: Maths Games 72

Chapter 8: Circle Games..90

Chapter 9: Physical Games...104

Chapter 10: Relay Games 114

Chapter 11: Early Phonics And Literacy Games...................118

About The Author

Martin Williams

Martin is the founder of the early years training company Early Impact. He has worked in the early years for ten years, teaching in both Preschool and Reception. He is driven by a determination to make early education exciting and engaging for both children and adults.

In his work with Early Impact, he has trained thousands of teachers and practitioners in many of the key areas of the early years. He has delivered school improvement projects for authorities, and he has led training for local early years quality teams.

He blogs and writes about all the educational topics he believes he can make a difference in, and he is strongly committed to sharing information and helping others as much as he can. You can find his blog by going to www.earlyimpactlearning.com

He is passionate about the 'practical' nature of learning both for adults and children. All of his courses are fast-paced, interactive, and contain a multitude of real-life resources that attendees try out.

He runs early years training courses in face-to-face venues across the North of England and the Midlands, specialising in early phonics, early maths, fine motor and mark-making. He delivers several online training sessions through Early Impact's website which you can find here - https://earlyimpactlearning.com/online-courses/

Introduction

These are crazy times to be living in! During this international pandemic very few things are clear. However, there is one thing that we know – social distancing in some form will be around to stay for the foreseeable.

Socially distancing with young children throws up multiple challenges and questions.

How much is social distancing possible with children? What age can children first start to understand it? How do we explain it? How do we help and support them with this lack of human connection? These are just some of the questions, and there will be so many more.

This book certainly does not provide all the answers, and it does not pretend to.

What it does provide is a clear and detailed description of 101 games that you can play with children between the ages of 3 to 7 that adhere (on paper at least!) to social distancing.

Over the past few weeks I have rooted around through the hundreds, probably thousands of games and activities I have tried out in the early years over the years, and tried to find the best of these that can be done with social distancing.

These are the content of this guide.

Wellbeing is at the heart of this book. Mental health amongst young children has been tested recently in a way that it has not been for generations.

I believe that during this phase of education that we are now in, wellbeing has to be first and foremost.

There is an element of wellbeing and mental health throughout every chapter in this book. These games and activities teach the core and simple skills of life, such as eye contact, teamwork, and listening and communication.

Even though I have split sections off into central areas of the curriculum, such as phonics and maths, these interpersonal skills underpin everything.

You cannot play these games all the time, and social distancing simply won't be possible continually. However, these games provide a snapshot of some time you can spend as a unit, practising social distancing in a fun and human-spirited context.

I believe outdoors is going to be a massive lifeline in these times, and so I have included huge numbers of outdoor games, and probably the vast majority of these 101 activities (possibly all) could be done outside.

Although most early years practitioners understand and have experienced the value in outdoor education, I hope this knowledge will transmit into the years above also. There seems to be a general consensus that outdoors is currently a safer environment from the perspective of transmission of infection. It offers greater space, and freedom to move. Also, many of its key benefits are what will be strongly required now more than ever – mental and physical health, independence, and human interaction.

In writing this book, a few challenges have been thrown up.

The main one of these is objects. I have tried to basically eliminate objects and resources from all of these activities.

This is just because of the risks of disease transmission through sharing objects.

This is very hard, as the early years is basically a resource-based curriculum. Trying to maintain the key levels of fun and engagement without resources takes a lot of creativity.

Just to be clear - I am not saying I would remove objects from your setting. It is just I have not used them in these games. A full curriculum in the early years without objects is impossible. This book does not provide a full provision overview, but just a snapshot of games to enhance it.

The only objects that do feature in this book will be used by an adult. Probably the only exceptions to this are some rubber spots which feature in lots of the games. The children will be sitting or standing on these, and not touching them with their hands (at least not much).

Also, there are some games where a rope or string is used, but the children will only hold one bit of it each.

Other than these, this book is 101 games without objects, but where imagination, movement, music, role play, storytelling, and many other skills come to the fore.

The other major challenge was trying to design games that kept the children two metres apart. I have used the idea of two metres throughout the book as the guideline set out in the UK. I know in other countries this is different – it is one metre in some, and 6 feet in others. Please just adapt this for your country.

Keeping two metres apart in games is certainly not natural, and has never really been done much before. Close human interaction has always been a major principle of the early years.

However, I have come up with 101 ideas in the end.

Some of the games are old classics. There are things like playground games, party games, and classic listening and memory games. Some have needed major tweaking to allow for social distancing, and I have tried to explain this as clearly as possible.

Other games I have invented, and are brand new for this book.

Others are adapted from games that are either pre-existing or invented, that I have used in phonics, maths, PE or outdoor games. They are games that teach skills across the curriculum that work really well despite keeping children apart.

A few disclaimers to get out of the way before I start...

This book is not about teaching social distancing. It is about games that will work because they have social distancing as part of their rules.

Using these games cannot guarantee that what you are doing is one hundred per cent safe.

Like all games in the early years, they will often go wrong! Children will end up sitting on top of each other, or run the wrong way and end it banging into each other. Where there are young children and movement, things will go wrong.

Reducing risk in your setting will be a combination of many factors, such as hand-washing, routines for dropping off and picking up, timetables for the day, and many other things. These are not included in this book.

Right, now that's out of the way, let's get cracking.

This book is for anyone that works in any kind of childcare or education setting with children between the ages of 3 to 7, but they will also work for children older than this as well.

I hope it will also be useful for junior sports coaches, and leaders of youth clubs and anything else like that.

There is not a single screen to be found in any of these games. Children will have been bombarded with screens possibly more than ever before over the recent period, and so now is the time to re-connect with the values of human interaction and comradeship.

This is a generation that will live through a period of life when the things valued in the past like socialising, hugging and physical proximity, are a cause of anxiety and fear.

We need to try to replicate some of the skills and experiences that otherwise might be lost in the safest framework that we can.

CHAPTER 1

Sitting In Pairs Games

This chapter contains a combination of some of the old classics, and also some pretty innovative activities as well. Most are great for a range of ages.

The idea here is that a pair of children are going to sit down facing each other (at two metres apart). If you do this outside, you could mark where to sit on the floor potentially.

This could be done with a small group of children, or for much larger groups, potentially up to at least 30. A large space is required for that many children to all be safely apart.

OK, here are the strategies:

1.'And Then' Story

Let's kick off with a fantastic storytelling activity.

This is realistically for children from about the age of 4 upwards (it will be trickier before this age).

The idea is that a pair of children sit facing each other (2 metres apart of course!)

One child is going to go first. They quite simply start a story. It can be on any theme they like – for example, 'One day a frog went into the forest.'

The next child is going to start their sentence 'And then...' and in such a way they will carry on the story. (For example, 'And then a witch flew down.')

Keep going like this: one sentence at a time, with the next child carrying it on by saying 'and then.'

Top Tips – Model it first, either with another willing adult, or at least a child with good communication skills. To make it easier, start them off with the opening line and they go from there. Before social distancing I used to get them to pass an object between each other after every sentence, but what I have described is the no-objects version.

2.Mirror Image

This is a fun game that introduces reflection and symmetry to an extent, as well as being great for eye contact and teamwork.

One child is the leader and the other child copies. Have a few goes then swop roles.

The leader is going to do some sort of movement, and the other child is going to copy. For example, they might lift their arm, and the other child lifts their arm. They wave, and the other child waves.

Children naturally will do this like a mirror, as in if one child waves their right arm, the other child waves their left.

Other actions they could do are things like moving their head from side to side, all sorts of different arm movements, clapping, patting their knees, and any other ideas they can come up with.

3.Counting Forwards/Backwards

A bit of maths now. This game is fantastic for practising rote counting.

The easiest way to do it is to start from 1, but you can extend it in multiple ways.

Basically, in its easiest form, one child will say 'one', then the other says 'two'. The first child says 'three' and so on. Keep counting for as long as they can.

Other ways to try this game are:

i) Starting from 0

ii) Counting on from a given number, e.g. 6

iii) Counting in silly voices (such as a witch, or an alien)

iv) Counting backwards from 5 or 10

v) Counting backwards from a given number, e.g. 7.

4.Count in 10s/2s/5s

A bit of a harder one now for children from probably about 6 upwards (although some 5 year olds will be able to do it too).

Count in different times tables, e.g. 2s, 5s or 10s (though it could really be anything).

Again, different ways to extend it include:

i) Count in 10s or 2s but start at a given number (e.g. 30)

ii) Count backwards

iii) Count backwards from a given number

iv) Count beyond the range of the times table that they know (e.g. beyond 12 lots of the number)

5.Staring Contest

The old classic staring contest!

This is the ultimate game for eye-contact, which is so important for children in these strange screen-obsessed times.

You simply sit staring at each other, and the child that holds off from blinking the longest is the champion.

You an also do the laughing version, where you stare and the winner is the one that doesn't laugh. Hours of fun.

6.Rock Paper Scissors

Another old classic from the repertoire.

I'm sure you know how to play this one, but just in case – two children sit opposite each other.

They have one hand in a fist. They 'beat' this into their other cupped hand as they say '1,2,3…' and on the fourth downwards motion they make either a rock (fist), paper (straight palm), or scissors (two fingers stretched out).

Rock beats scissors, and loses to paper.

Scissors beats paper, and loses to rock.

Paper beats rock, and loses to scissors.

Keep your score! You can play best of 3 or best of 5 (or more).

Top Tip – For older children of probably about 7 upwards, there is a harder version of the game called 'Rock Paper Scissors Spock Lizard'. In this 'Spock' is signified by a Vulcan split fingered salute, and 'lizard' by a kind of sock puppet hand.

Take a deep breath, because here are the rules…

Spock beats scissors and rock, but loses to paper and lizard.

Lizard beats spock and paper, but loses to rock and scissors.

Rock beats scissors and lizard, but loses to paper and spock.

Paper beats rock and spock, but loses to scissors and lizard.

Scissors beats paper and lizard, but loses to rock and spock.

Good luck getting your head around that one!

7. Team Rock Paper Scissors

My son told me about this variation that he did at school. Probably for children aged 6 upwards this one.

This is a standing game, rather than a sitting one.

The idea of this (breaking slightly from the theme of pairs) is that you have a circle of children, all standing 2m apart. It could be anywhere between 3 to about 6 players max.

Once again, you all go '1,2,3,' then show your rock, paper or scissors. If all three are shown then you just go again. But if just two are shown, then the losers are out and sit down.

Then whoever is left will go again. At the end there will be one winner.

Then all stand up and go again.

8.Make The Number

This is a game for children of about 5 upwards.

Two players face each other, and the adult gives them a number. They are going to try to make the number by sharing it between them by holding out their fingers.

So, for example, if the number is '8', then one child might be holding out '5' fingers and the other child will try to find '3'.

This takes lots of thinking and time in reality. The big rule is that one child can't make the number by themselves. You have to share!

Excellent for practical number bonds and problem solving.

9.Yes/No Game

This is slightly trickier than some of these other pairs games, and I probably wouldn't try this with children under the age of 5.

This game is well known on many kid's youtube channels, so many children will know how to do this. It is also a popular playground game.

You simply talk to each other and try to make the other person say 'yes' or 'no'. You can use any tactics you want.

The main one is to think of questions that the other person cannot avoid answering without saying 'yes' or 'no'. A very amusing game to watch when it is working well.

Again it is great for communication, listening and creativity.

10.Can't Laugh Challenge

This is a great game for some good old-fashioned fun, as well as requiring eye-contact and creativity as well.

Many children have seen this game on Youtube, Tik Tok, or something similar to that.

One child basically sits there and is not allowed to speak. The other one is going to try to make them laugh.

They can use any silly comments, foolish faces, funny noises – anything they can think of. A good team-building game and excellent for confidence.

When that child has succeeded in making them laugh, they switch roles.

Top Tips – Comedy is a hard thing to explain to some children, and there will be some that just don't know what to do. Others will just find everything hilarious. Like all these games, there is no easy quick fix that will work perfectly for everyone, but playing it a few times will help children learn from others.

11.Copy The Face

This is a quick game that is good for eye contact, and an understanding of human emotion.

One child is going to be the leader to start with, and the other is going to copy. The leader makes different facial expressions – happy, sad, cross, shocked etc. The other one tries to copy.

Then after they have had a go at that way round, get them to swop roles.

If you want to make it easier, then the adult could lead the children by telling them the emotion to try, such as 'let's all do a cross face'. This is the simpler version of the game.

CHAPTER 2

Chalk on the Floor Games

Now for a few games that I have more or less invented afresh with the idea of social distancing as a starting point. I suppose some of them are based on pre-existing games but are just re-framed within the new context of keeping apart from each other.

You need some chalk for these and a large concrete surface.

They all involve drawing some markings on the floor that vary from game to game.

This hopefully makes social distancing fun for at least a few minutes, and not just a continual chore.

OK, here we go…

1.Swop Places

Markings Required – some square boxes drawn all over the place in a random assortment. Each will be 2m from the others. You need at least as many boxes as you have children, and a few extra is probably a good idea.

A nice easy game to kick us off.

Every child starts by standing in one box each. The adult then shouts out who should swop boxes. Say things like 'Swop if you are a girl.' 'Swop if you have black hair.' 'Swop if you support (X football team).'

Each time, a number of children will be swopping round their places.

You can make this one trickier in a few ways which include:

i) Create a combination of two or more features. For example, 'Swop places if you are a boy and you like apples.'

ii) Include phonics, such as the sounds that children's names start with (e.g. 'Swop places if your name begins with 'm'.)

iii) The children take turns to create their own criteria for swopping

2. Shark Attack

Markings Required – Same as the last game. Some square boxes drawn in a random assortment, each 2m apart.

The adult holds some kind of instrument for this one. Something like a drum would be perfect.

The children are going to move in different ways all around the space this time, trying to stay a reasonable distance away from others if they can. They are in shark-infested waters so watch out!

At any given moment you are going to hit the instrument. This is the sound of the shark!

When they hear it they are going to run and find a box. When you are in the box you are safe. This is the life-boat.

It's as simple as that.

Ways to really bring it to life include:

i) Move in lots of different ways around the space – hop, jump, skip, slither etc

ii) Children select how the group will move

iii) Maybe swim like different fish

3. Box Jumpers

Marking Required – Same as the first two games

This one combines movement with simple one-to-one counting.

Pick a way to move, e.g. jumping. Everyone is going to start in one box, but then try to get to another box by jumping. As they jump they are going to count how many they do.

Try different actions, such as hopping, sideways jump, or big giant strides.

4. Asteroid

Markings Required – Same as the first two games

This is a bit like 'What's The Time Mr Wolf?'

Everyone starts in a box, and the adult says a number of steps they can take out of the box, for example '2'. They stride twice out of the box. Then say another number, and they take that number of steps extra.

Keep going like this, until you shout 'Asteroid!'

At that moment they need to run back to the same box they were in. This is the underground cave, safe from any asteroids. They have five seconds – do a countdown '5,4,3,2,1,0.' If they get back in time they are safe.

You could potentially do a competitive version, where if they didn't get back in time they had to go and sit somewhere in a socially distanced line at the side of the game.

5. Number Swop

Markings required – Boxes or circles in a random assortment, each with one number written in the middle of it. There need to be at least two of each number, though there could be more than that (e.g. four boxes with number '6' in would be fine). You also require a lot more boxes than there are children.

This is a great game for recognising numbers, and can also be adapted for other things like sounds or tricky words.

One child stands in one box each to start with. Simply shout a number – e.g. '7'. Everyone that is standing in a circle or square with a 7 written in it are going to run and find a new box. The big rule is that you can't run to another box with a 7 in it – you've got to find a new number.

Keep going with different numbers!

There are many ways of adapting this game which include:

i) Making number bonds, for example of 10. Say things like 'What do you add to 3 to make 10?' Everyone in the '7' box runs to another.

ii) Put sounds, tricky words, or CVCs in the box

iii) Try one more or one less of a number – e.g. 'What is one less than 3?' Everyone in a '2' will swop places

6. Team Jump

Markings Required – A line of circles, a bit like stepping stones in a row. Each circle will be about a metre wide, and they will all be about a metre apart from each other in a long line.

This is one of those games that uses one of the ultimate concepts – the floor is lava! Children really love this, and some will play these lava games for hours.

You can't stand on the lava, but you can stand on the circles because they are the stepping stones. Phew!

The tricky bit for this is starting off in a socially distanced straight line. Much easier said than done.

The first child is going to stand in the opening circle. Then they will try to jump to the next stepping stone (without any feet going in the dreaded lava).

As soon as they are on the next stepping stone, the second child will step onto the first stepping stone.

Keep going like this! The circles could be in a straight line (as I described at the start), or you could also have them in a wide circle, or in a snake shape around the yard.

To make it harder, you can only stand on one leg.

7. Sounding Out Words Jumping

Markings Required – Three circles in a row with a bit of a gap in between each circle. These have one letter in each circle that make up a CVC word, e.g. 's-i-t' making the word 'sit'. Have lots of these circles all over the place, so lots of children can have a go at one time.

This is a fun and active blending game.

The idea is that a child jumps across the three stepping stones, saying the sound of the letter that they land on each time. For example, they jump and go 's-i-t.' Then they take one final jump off the last stepping stone and say the word 'sit'.

They then go and find another word and repeat. Lots of children can be doing this all over the place without the need to be going too close to each other.

This can be made harder in these ways:

i) Use four circles, or even five for longer words.

ii) Use words with digraphs and trigraphs in. It is a good idea to use one phoneme per circle, a bit like a phoneme frame

iii) You could write simple captions in the circles, e.g. 'I can run' written across three stepping stones. They read the sentence as they jump.

8. Follow The Order

Markings Required – circles all over the place that are 2m apart. They will have the numbers in from 0 to 20, one number in each circle, but in a random array.

This is a fun and practical ordering numbers game.

Start with a socially distanced line of children next to number one. The first child stands in the number one circle, and then runs off to find number two. Then they go to number three etc.

The next child follows, then the next, and keep going like this.

You can adapt this in many ways, including:

i) Make it much easier. You could start with the numbers 1-5

ii) Go backwards – start at 10 or 20

iii) Try starting from a random number such as 7, and either going forwards or backwards

CHAPTER 3

Memory Games

Developing memory has a huge number of benefits across the whole child and can impact the entire curriculum.

Increasing memory skills has a positive impact on:

    i)   Increased phonic and reading ability

    ii) A heightened ability to make sense of their lives

    iii) Children are able to retain knowledge better across all areas

    iv) Increased skills in listening and attention

Many of these games you can do with a range of ages – just vary the difficulty depending on age and skill.

Many of these memory games have died out, or are definitely on the decline. Classic games that used to be played by families as they drove on day trips, for example, are played now very rarely.

Anyway, here are the memory games:

1.Missing Child Game

The children sit in a socially distanced circle. One child is selected to come and sit in the middle. They are going to close their eyes (and probably put their hands over their eyes as well to reduce the risk of cheating).

Then pick one child to go and hide. You can do this by pointing at the child silently. They will go off and hide somewhere, for example behind a table, cupboard or door. Somewhere where they can't be seen is the big idea.

Then the child in the middle opens their eyes and tries to guess who has gone missing. A great game for eye-contact and remembering who sits where.

In the past, I have played this game as a more interactive version, where everyone closes their eyes. You then select a child to go and hide, and then everyone opens their eyes to guess who's missing.

I used to tap them on the shoulder. If you can find a way round this, for example maybe touching them on the shoulder with a magic wand, then this is a great way to play this game.

2.Jungle Story – Adult Touches Objects

This is a classic memory game.

Smaller numbers are good for this game. Realistically under 10 is best, and probably about five or six children would be perfect.

This is a game where only the adult will be touching the objects. You require some kind of box or bag, and a few toy jungle animals.

Sit in a socially distanced circle. Take an animal out of the bag, for example a lion, and the first child will say, 'At the zoo we saw a lion.'

Then take another animal out, for example a crocodile. The next child in the circle will say 'At the zoo we saw a lion and a crocodile.'

Keep going in this vein.

There are two different versions of the game, an easy and harder.

For the easy version, keep the animals out on show so the children can see them.

The harder version, which is definitely the way to go for children aged four and up, is to show the animal briefly then put it into a bag or box. This way the children have to remember the animal sequence in their heads.

Top Tip – Give lots of clues and encouragement if they get stuck

3.Rhyming Train

For this game you need some rhyming pictures that are going to just be handled by an adult. This game is probably for children from the age of 3 upwards, although the harder version is definitely for those much older.

Have pictures of objects that all rhyme – for example, 'bat', 'cat', 'pat', 'hat', 'rat', 'mat'. Have at least the number of pictures you have children, and it is fine to have more than one picture of the same thing. For example, if you have 10 children, then it is fine to have two 'bats', two 'cats' etc, up to a total of 10 cards. This is another game, I would say, where fewer children are better.

Sit in a socially distanced circle. Show the pictures first just to check they know what all the things are.

For the easy game, take a card out and put it in front of you. The first person in the circle says what it is, e.g. 'hat'.

Then take another card out and put it next to that one. The next child says the first card and the second, for example 'hat, bat'. Then the next child says three – 'hat, bat, cat'. Keep going like this!

For the medium version difficulty of the game, take a card out but then put it into a box so they can't see it. This becomes much more of a memory challenge, keeping the words in their heads.

The hardest version of the game is where the children just make up the words themselves. This is only possible when children are able to confidently invent words that rhyme (realistically from 5 or 6 upwards for most children).

Rhyme is not the easy skill many people think it is! It is a very difficult concept, and hopefully one day will be recognised as such in education.

4. Magic Trick (Version of Kim's Game)

A great game to play with even very young children and all the way up to 7 or 8 year olds. Just vary the difficulty.

This is a jazzed-up version of the classic memory game 'Kim's Game.'

It is another one that will require a few objects that are handled by the adult. You also need a sheet, and a magic wand is optional but really does bring this activity to life.

Sit in a circle, and show the children a few objects sat next to each other. It could be a dog, horse and cow. It is a good idea to stick to a theme, I think, so it could be food, or animals, or superheroes for example. It is great to tap into their interests if you can, so superhero figures would probably be a great one.

They look at the objects, then cover them up with the sheet. Now for the magic!

Get the children to close their eyes (or the magic won't work!) and remove one object from under the sheet and hide it behind your back.

Then they open their eyes, and you take the sheet away. What's gone missing?

This is the easy version with just three objects, but you can increase this based on how well the children are doing. There is no limit to the number of objects you could potentially have.

Other ways to alter the game include:

i)   Have rhyming objects

ii) Have objects that begin with the same sound

iii) Remove two objects at a time

iv) Add an object!

5. What Did You Change?

This is a socially-distanced variation of a game that they really enjoy.

For this you need some pieces of clothing that the adult is going to put on. Things that can be put on or taken off quickly are good – for example, a hat, a coat, sunglasses, a scarf, and gloves would be perfect. It is great if you have a few different types of each piece of clothing, for example three hats, three sets of glasses etc.

This is another great one for 3-year olds upwards.

Basically the idea is that everyone sits in a socially distanced circle. The adult puts one version of all the clothes on. Then the children close their eyes.

The adult will take off one bit of clothing, and swap it for a different one. For example, they take off a cap, and put on a top hat.

Then the children open their eyes. What has been changed?

They find this hilarious.

Some changes are more subtle, such as one glove. Some more obvious – like a coat or hat. Sometimes just taking one off (like the scarf) and not putting anything else back on can trick them.

The version I used to play of this is where a child is in the middle of the circle, and they try different things on.

6.Picnic Game

Another classic memory game from yesteryear.

Have a picnic hamper (or box of some sort) and some food which can be either real or pretend.

Take a piece of food out, for example a cake, and the first person in the circle says 'For the picnic we take a cake.'

Get another piece of food out, for example a sandwich, and the next person says 'For the picnic we take a cake and a sandwich.'

Keep going like this.

This is another game where it is wise to limit the numbers to maybe about 6-8 max (if you can!)

The medium difficulty version is of course take them out and then put them back in so the children have to remember the foods in their minds.

The harder version is that they make up the food themselves.

7. Number String

Just to warn you, this game is a bit trickier than most of these other memory games.

Probably for children from the age of about 6 upwards.

Sit the children in a socially distanced circle. Then the first child is going to say a number between 0 and 10, for example '4'. Then the next child will say that number, and then also say one of their own between 0 and 10. So they might say, '4, 6'. The next child will say '4, 6, 9.'

Keep going like this until they can go on no longer.

Top Tip – As they say the numbers the adult can write them down on a large piece of paper that the children can't see. If anyone gets stuck, you can quickly show them the sequence to keep the game going.

8. What's In The Noisy Box?

This is a classic mix of a listening and memory game all rolled into one. Great for children from 3 upwards.

You require some kind of bag or box for this, and some kind of noisy objects. It could be something like a squeaky dog toy, a crisp packet, or a plastic bottle.

Put one of these objects into the bag or box first. Make sure the children haven't seen what's in there.

The children sit in a socially distanced circle. Make the noise of the thing in the box or bag. You could shake it, or put your hand in and squeeze it. Whatever it takes to get the object to make a noise.

Then you go round the circle and one at a time everyone guesses what it is that is making the noise.

When everyone has had a go, it is time for the memory challenge. Say things like 'Who said that it was a dog's toy?' (Everyone points to that person hopefully). 'Who said it was a toy duck?'

Then it's time for the big reveal!

Top Tip – you may want to make a quick note as you go round the circle to help you remember yourself what each child says.

CHAPTER 4

Listening Games

R ight, onto an absolute classic of the repertoire – listening games.

All of these games are excellent for even very young children, but can be adapted and used with older ones as well.

Listening skills have a huge impact across the whole curriculum as we know, but just to pick one area in particular: the link between listening skills and phonic development is massive! I know this has always been understood at phase one, but it definitely shouldn't just stop there. These listening games have a huge impact on children beyond that.

Start as easy as you possibly can with the young ones, but many of these activities are all infinitely expandable.

There are some favourite party games thrown into the mix here, as well as some good old solid listening games, and some brand new ones as well.

1.Wonky Donkey

A less well-known one (but a real gem!) to start with.

The children sit in a wide circle (all at least 2m apart). Pick one child to stand in the middle of the circle. They are the 'wonky donkey' and they put their hands over their eyes.

Then silently pick one child (probably by pointing). They are going to stand up and say 'Wonky Donkey'. Then they sit back down.

The wonky donkey will then wake up. They are allowed to open their eyes and have three guesses to say who it was that said 'wonky donkey'.

This is a voice recognition game. If you know what your friend's sound like, then you will be able to guess.

Also, it is thinking about where the sound has come from.

To make the game harder you can do some of the following:

i) Move round the circle before saying 'wonky donkey' and then creep back to your place

ii) Use a silly voice (like a monster)

iii) Whisper

Top Tip – before social distancing, I used to get the wonky donkey to hold a fake 'tail'. The child that was chosen then comes out and waggles the tail whilst saying 'wonky donkey'. This really adds to the fun.

2.Noisy Neighbour

This is an old chestnut from the archives, and one that children really love.

Have a feely bag or a box, and some objects that have been selected because they make a noise. They are what the noisy neighbour is going to use in his house to irritate the neighbours!

A top tip is to show the children what the objects are first, and also make the noise for them. This gives them a fighting chance of guessing what they are later.

Some good objects are things like a crisp packet, a plastic bag, a brush, a dog toy, bells – and anything else like that.

There is a chant that goes like this:

Noisy Neighbour!

Noisy Neighbour!

Stop that noise!

Then put your hand into the bag and make the noise of one of the objects.

The children try to guess what it is. It's as simple as that.

Probably start with only about 3 or 4 objects, but as they get better at the game you can expand the number you use.

Top Tip - The harder version of the game is not to show them the objects first, but just let them guess. This is significantly trickier though, just to warn you.

3.Odd One Out

This game is not as easy as it looks. There are also quite a few different ways to play it.

One version is a simple listening game. You tell a story, but it has one element in it that makes no sense.

For example, 'For dinner I ate chicken, a sausage, a leopard, carrots and potatoes.' What sounds a bit ridiculous in that sentence?

You could also have some objects, handled by the adult.

For example, 'Let's see what's in the car park. We have a tractor, truck, car, toothbrush, motorbike.'

The harder version of the game is where you have objects that share a more complex association.

It could be rhyming objects, for example. You might have a cat, hat, bat and dog. Which is the odd one out?

It could also be words that start with the same sound, are the same colour, or some other feature like that.

4. What's In The Box Phonecall

This is a simple listening game that is really jazzed up by using some kind of pretend phonecall.

Have a box or bag with some mystery objects inside. You also have a pretend phone of some sort (which is optional but really does bring it to life).

The idea is that you are going to describe what is in the box and the children are going to guess. But to make it much more exciting, someone (or something) is going to phone you up.

It could be the Big Bad Wolf. It could be a witch or an alien. Maybe a character from a story you were doing at the time would be a good choice.

Anyway, the character phones up and describes an object. Make it as exciting as you can! What a shock the character has phoned! What's that?! You have left objects in your magic bag!? For us!?

An example of the description could be 'It's an animal. It has four legs. It is grey with a trunk. It has large ears.' (It's an elephant)

Objects could be animals, food, toys, or random objects from around the room.

Top Tip – Another variation is that instead of a phonecall, get a puppet to describe what is in the box.

5.Musical Statues On A Spot

Rubber spots are one of the few resources I have included in this book for the children to interact with. They will not be touching them with their hands, and I think they are going to be really useful for marking out spaces and keeping children apart in games such as this.

I am sure that everyone knows this musical statues game.

All you do is space out the rubber spots across the area you are going to use so that they are at least 2m apart. Children are going to be moving and dancing in that one space.

When the music stops – they freeze! If you see them move then they have to sit down.

You can do it so you get a winner at the end, or just the more non-competitive version where you have a few goes and then everyone stands back up.

6.Musical Bumps On The Spot

This is a similar idea to Musical Statues. This is another game that is ideal for younger children (probably 3-5).

Arrange the spots in the same random array to aid social distancing. Then put some music on and the children all dance. When it stops, they sit down straight away on their spot. The slowest person is eliminated (if you are doing the competitive version.) For non-competitive, just have another go.

A classic party game that is good for simple listening skills. A perfect combo.

7. Where's That Sound?

You need at least a couple of instruments for this one, that will be played by either one adult or possibly even two.

Have a circle of socially-distanced children. Get them all to close their eyes.

You are going to have an instrument, for example a tambourine, walk quietly around the circle and then stop and shake it. The idea is the children are going to point to where the sound is coming from.

Then move to another point in the circle, and repeat.

You can make this game much harder in a few different ways. Some of these include:

i) Play the instrument really quietly

ii) Have two adults with instruments at different parts of the circle. Then the children have to point with two hands

iii) Play two instruments both really quietly

iv) Play two instruments that are the same (e.g. two tambourines). This makes it quite a bit trickier

v) Use three instruments! Children point with two hands and maybe one foot

vi) Guess what the instruments are also

8. Noisy Box!

This is a really fun one for young children in particular.

You have some kind of box for this one, and a few things inside that make a noise. The adult is going to handle these. The children sit in a socially distanced circle.

The objects could be a representation of something that makes a noise in reality – they don't have to actually make it. So, for example, you could have a toy chicken in the box, because chickens make noises in real life.

The idea of this is that the adult looks in the box first, and picks an object (but doesn't show it). They make the noise of the object. Then everyone tries to copy!

You can go 'round the circle'. In this the adult makes the noise to the first person in the circle. They copy and pass it on to the next person, and keep going like this all the way round. Then everyone tries to guess what it is.

Some great objects to use might be:

i)   Toy animals – this is probably the easiest way to do it and a good way to start

ii) Things that make electric sounds like a phone, or alarm clock

iii) DIY tools, like a hammer or drill

iv) Noisy objects, like a plastic bag, or tin foil. (This is a much harder version of the game)

CHAPTER 5

Rope Or String Games

This shorter chapter was inspired by the VE Day celebrations I saw recently. A huge line of people were doing a socially distanced conga at a park somewhere in London.

They did this by holding onto a giant rope, each 2m apart from the others.

This got me thinking, and so here are some socially distanced rope games.

For these you need to have some kind of long rope or string.

You can mark off some 2m markings on it with something like duct tape that is cut into small pieces and twisted round at different points.

A quick note on the type of rope: a smooth rope would work well to avoid any friction burns. You don't want anything too coarse. You could use:

i)   A long piece of string

ii) A long piece of wool

iii) Some long skipping ropes tied together

iv) A long but quite smooth rope

These games are good to play on grass if you have any. It is also a good idea to keep number reasonably low for many of these games.

1.Follow The Leader

This is really simple, and this is the kind of activity you will see many children doing in child-led play in forest schools.

The more you can tap into the natural interests and instincts of children the better.

All you do is all hold the rope at 2m points (probably marked on by some sort of tape). The leader leads the way, and you walk around the setting in a long line. Every now and then, change leader.

You could potentially go on a quest or a treasure hunt like this. There may be little signs hidden round the outside area, or cards put up on the fences or on the wall. It could be something simple like trying to find different shapes or numbers.

Older children could have written clues, like 'look on the bench' or 'go to the bin.'

Going quite slowly is important in all these rope games to avoid injury.

2. Rope Train

This is a fantastic one for train lovers, and there are always loads of those in the early years. My son was completely obsessed with trains at this age, although he's not even remotely interested in them now that he has reached the grand old age of 9.

Start with one child at the head of the rope. This is the train driver.

The driver is going to drive the train around the 'track'. This can be wherever you want – it could be to the fence and back, or a lap of the field or yard, or you could mark a wide circle on the floor with cones.

Whilst the driver drags the rope around the track, the other children wait in a socially distanced line, one behind the other. They are the carriages waiting at the station. Probably about 5 carriages would be a sensible maximum number.

When one lap is completed, the next 'carriage' will hold onto the rope 2 metres behind the driver, and then they will both set off on another lap.

Next time they come back, they will pick another carriage up. At the end all the carriages will be behind the train.

Great for cooperation, teamwork, and a bit of discipline also in waiting for the train.

3. Movement Train

This one is an absolute classic. One of the all-time great early phonics games with a rope added to it.

You can have anywhere from 3 children to probably about ten.

All the children hold the rope at two metre points. They are the 'train'.

The adult goes at the front of the children. This time the adult is the 'driver.'

You need a few instruments for this one. Pick one instrument to start with, let's say a drum.

The idea is that the adult walks at the front of the train playing the drum. The children in the train are going to follow, and move in a way that suits the sound. So, for example, they might stamp round like giants for the drum, be on their tip-toes for a triangle, or shake their hips for a maraca.

You can vary the speed and the loudness of the instrument. So, for example, you can play the drum really loud and get them stamping away, but then change to really quiet and they start sneaking.

You can play quickly and get them moving that way, or slow it down for longer and more deliberate movements.

The perfect outdoor instrument game for social distancing!

4. Jump In A Line

This is another quite simple one. All you need is the rope again, and some children holding it.

Whoever is the leader is going to decide how to move. It might be jumping, or hopping, going low, or going high with the rope held up.

Just keep the movements slow and sure to avoid injuries.

5. Conga!

This is probably best led by an adult with a few children behind them on the rope.

I'm sure you know the song, but it basically goes:

Let's all do the conga!

Let's all do the conga!

Na nah nah nah! Hey!

Na nah nah nah! Hey!

On the first 'hey' you kick one leg out to the side, then on the next you kick the other leg out on the other side.

6. Balance Rope

For this one you quite simply put the rope down on the floor and the children create a socially-distanced line. One at a time they try to walk along it like a balance beam.

You could put the rope in a straight line, or it could be in a wiggly line.

CHAPTER 6

Classic Outdoor Games (With A Twist)

There is a huge emphasis on the outdoors in this book, so I thought I should include a chapter on some classic outside games.

All of these either involve social distancing anyway, or they can be tweaked just slightly to make it work.

Games that have stood the test of time across generations and different countries and cultures will always go down a storm as they have some of the magic ingredients that fire up children's imaginations.

1.Shadow Tag

This is definitely the best version of tag for social distancing.

It's a very simple concept – one person is 'it' and chases the others. The way to 'tag' someone is to stamp on their shadow. If your shadow is stood on then you are now 'it'.

There are different versions you can play (like almost all of these games)…

For example, you can do it where you start with a few children being 'it'.

Another way is that you start with either one or several children as 'it' and then every time they stand on someone's shadow, that person joins the 'it' team. In the end you will have just a couple of children running for their lives against a whole team. This way, you can also have a 'winner' at the end.

One thing to look out for in this game is disputes! (Just to warn you) It is not always as clear cut as normal tag when you actually have been 'tagged' and some children will bend the rules slightly.

Conflict resolution, however, is a critical part of play and of life in general.

Top Tip – Strictly speaking, it might not be best to play this one around mid-day when our shadows are shortest. Ideally, longer shadows are better, such as you get in the morning or afternoon to keep children roughly two metres apart.

2. Blind Man's Buff - Pairs

I think this is a classic Victorian game, and one that can be played in many different ways.

It's best not to use a blindfold for this (for hygiene), but rather just get children to close their eyes, and putting their hands over their eyes also works well to avoid cheating.

There are a few variations of Blind Man's Buff which are all brilliant for social distancing, but here is the first…

Children are in pairs. The child with their eyes closed is at the front, and the other walks two metres behind them. The child at the back tries to direct them to a certain point, for example, to a tree, or a bench. This is great for positional language – things like go forward, left, right, back, and all that kind of thing.

Be aware of safety! Encourage them to walk slowly, and it is best done in a reasonably deserted space so they don't bang into others.

3. Blind Man's Buff - Target

Here's another variation of Blind Man's Buff.

The children sit in a socially distanced circle. Pick one to stand in the middle of the circle and close their eyes.

The adult draws a 'target' somewhere in the circle with chalk on the ground. It could be a circle, or it could be a cross – either will work.

The idea now is that one child in the circle is going to have a go at directing the child with their eyes closed to move towards the target. The idea is to try to get them to stand on the target.

Once again it is great for all sorts of positional language – forwards, backwards, sideways – and also counting and predicting. Children will be saying things like 'Go forward 7 steps.' Lots of thinking and problem solving will be happening.

4. Pin The Tail On The Donkey

Inspired by that last Blind Man's Buff game, I thought this would be a good variation of Pin The Tail On The Donkey.

This is another good game to play in pairs, though it could also be a circle game.

One child is on, and will close their eyes, the other child is going to help them.

For this game, the adult will have drawn a large donkey on the ground. You could have several donkeys all over the place for teams of children to play it at the same time.

One child will direct the other to stand in the right place for the donkey's tail – on its bottom basically. There is no real tail involved; it is just a case of standing in the right place.

5. Hide And Seek

It probably needs no introduction this one, but just for the record, here we go...

One person is 'on'. They stand somewhere and count to a specified number. Everyone else goes to hide.

Then the person that is on says 'Coming to find you!' and goes to find them.

When you are found, you traditionally join the other person in searching for the rest. Remember to stay two metres apart during this bit of the game!

This game taps into the enthusiasm children have for an element of danger, and of feeling lost or hidden temporarily.

6. Sardines

This is a variation of Hide and Seek, and one that does take a bit of tweaking to the original rules in order to adhere to social distancing.

The idea of this game is that just one person goes to hide first of all. The other children are all 'it'. They will have to stand in some kind of socially distanced array – maybe a line or a circle.

They count in a group to a specified number. This is an excellent game for practising rote counting in a practical and purposeful way.

Then they all say, 'Coming to find you' and go off separately to look for the person hiding.

When one child finds the one that is hiding, that child will then join then. The big thing now is to encourage the children to stay two metres apart when they find the other one. If they can't join them exactly where they are hiding (for instance if it was behind a bin) then they just try and hide somewhere close.

Then when another child finds them, they hide somewhere near as well.

In the end all the children will hiding close to each other (though not too close!)

7. Floor Is Lava

This concept will definitely come up in other games as well, as many children are obsessed with the idea of the ground being lava!

However, here it is a simple obstacle course.

There are different ways to play it. One way could be a simple 'chalk on the ground' game. You draw an obstacle course. The adult could do this, or potentially children could as well.

Draw different shapes and 'obstacles' that the children can jump over and balance along. For example, some designs could be:

i) Several circles with gaps in between in a row

ii) A long thin rectangle like a balance beam to walk along

iii) Shapes with big gaps in between to jump over

iv) Zig-zag or wavy lines to follow

Another way of doing this activity is building a simple obstacle course with things like pallets, crates, ropes, rubber spots, and anything else you can find.

They walk over it, making sure not to touch the lava.

8. Red Light Green Light

This game just takes a bit of tweaking to make it fully compatible with social distancing.

The basic idea is that one child is the traffic light. They stand quite a way from the other children. The rest all start in a socially distanced line, usually next to a wall or fence.

The variation from the normal game that would work is to draw two circles on the floor, at least two metres apart. One of these circles is for the traffic light to stand in, the other is going to be in between the traffic light and the other children, about 2m in front of the traffic light. This is the circle that the other children are going to try to get to.

The traffic light turns their back on the other children, and shouts, 'Green light!' This is the cue for the other children to start sneaking towards them.

Whenever they feel like it, the traffic light will spin round and say 'Red light!' If they see anyone move, then they tell them to go back to the start.

The winner is the person that stands on the circle first.

9. Mother May I?

This one works well if the adult is the 'mother' in the game, but with a bit of practice children are able to do it OK as well (hopefully!).

The same set-up is required as for Red Light, Green Light. You have two circles on the ground, one for the 'mother' to stand in, and the other in front of the other circle, that the children are going to try to get to.

All the children start in a socially distanced line facing the 'mother'.

The idea is that one at a time a child will ask if they can move in a certain way. For example, they might say 'Can I go four steps forward?'

It is up to the 'mother' to say 'yes' or 'no'.

If the mother says 'no', then she can tell them where to go, for example 'go five steps back.'

Common requests are things like 'steps', 'jumps', or 'hops'.

The winner is the first person to get to the circle. The 'mother' is very much in control of who wins in this game, so it's good to share it around (obviously) if that's you.

10. What's The Time Mr Wolf? (Shadow Tag)

Here's another classic that just takes a little tweak to make it work. The tweak is to incorporate shadow tag into it, instead of the traditional tagging of children with the hand.

There is one group of children, who stand socially distanced in a line, and then there is one of them that will be Mr Wolf. The wolf stands away from the others. To start with the wolf has his back turned to the others.

The children in the group all say, 'What's the time, Mr Wolf?'

The wolf turns round and says a time, such as 'Five o'clock.' Then he turns back away from them, as the children do five footsteps towards him.

They ask again – 'What's the time, Mr Wolf?'

The wolf keeps on giving them times, and then turns away. At some point the wolf will say, 'It's dinner time!'

At this point the wolf will chase the children as they try to run back to where they started. If the wolf shadow tags one of them, then they will be the wolf next time round.

CHAPTER 7

Maths Games

I've had to limit myself to 14 games for this chapter, though I could have really gone for it and created many more.

But these are the cream of the crop, that I promise you will get a lot out of.

There are a few barriers in the way of teaching maths in a socially distanced context, probably the biggest being that maths learning is driven by objects.

You teach it through using playdough, found objects, loose parts, manipulating interesting real-life resources, and lots of other strategies like that which require continually touching and interacting with *things*.

Well, that's all been thrown out of the window, and these are games that require virtually no objects (or at least only those held by an adult). I have tried to cover as many skills as I can think of as well, to give a reasonably broad curriculum coverage, although different types of counting do figure quite highly in this list.

Pretty much all of these games are great either outside or inside, and the choice is yours.

Here we go…

1.Clock-Face

Key Skills: Number recognition, and can be adapted for one more or one less.

The children stand in a wide socially distanced circle for this one. Putting rubber spots down at 2m intervals in a circle would be perfect for this game.

Have some number cards, and the adult puts one number quite near to each spot in a way that it can clearly be read from the spot. Use numbers that are relevant to your children, so if you're only learning 1-5 then use those, but it could be 0-20 or whatever else.

If you have a source of music then that is great, or alternatively you can just tell them to 'stop'. Anyway, what you do is start the music, and the children move in the same direction around the circle.

Then the music stops, and the children stand on the nearest circle to them. They say the number they are stood next to.

Then repeat.

Nice ways to jazz it up include:

i)   Say the number in different voices, for example like a ghost or a princess

ii)   Say the number in your 'fast' voice, i.e. if it was 'nine', then say 'nine nine nine nine...' as fast as you can

iii) Say one more of a number

iv) Say one less

2. Swop Places

Key Skills: Number recognition, cooperation, one more or less, addition, subtraction

Sit in a circle again, and the adult will have two matching sets of number cards. Place one number card on the ground in front of each child. There will be two children that have a '5' next to them, two that have '3', and so on.

Once again, if you are trying to teach higher numbers then use these.

It's a nice simple one this game: the adult shouts a number and the two children that are sitting next to the number jump up and run around the outside of the circle. You could potentially mark a wide circle out with cones for them to run around, to keep them 2m away from everyone else.

They get to where the other number is and sit down next to it.

Then try another number.

Once again, this can be extended in several ways, including:

i)   Finding one more or less

ii) Using number bonds, e.g. 'What number goes with 3 to make five.'

iii) Addition, such as 'What is three add two'

iv) Subtraction – 'What is six subtract four.'

3. Number/Shape Dive

Key Skills: Number recognition, shape recognition, one more/less, addition/subtraction

The children sit in a circle.

In the middle of the circle have some numbers or some shapes. Drawing them on the floor with chalk would be an easy way of achieving this.

Led by the adult, everyone in the circle is going to say '1,2,3...' and then you're going to say a child's name and also a number (or shape) to stand on. For example, you might say 'Charlie, 6!' Charlie would jump up, run over and stand on number six, and then go back to where they were sitting.

When they have a good idea of how to play it, you can nominate a child to pick who will jump up and also what they will stand on.

This game could also be done for:

    i)   Addition – Say, 'Charlie – four add four.' (And subtraction is the same principle)

ii) For one more or one less, e.g. 'Charlie, what is one less than six?'

iii) For 3D shapes if you can find or draw pictures

iv) For tricky words or sounds

v) For something like pictures of animals or pictures of emotion faces for really young children

4. Action Dice

Key Skills: Number recognition, one to one counting, rote counting

Unlike the vast majority of the activities in this book, this one takes just a little preparation. You basically need two big dice.

You could use those foam dice with pockets in the side, or you can now get whiteboard dice that you write straight onto. I use two wooden dice that look like wooden blocks. Anything like this will be fine.

On one dice you write some numbers 1-6, and on the other you draw some pictures that represent actions that the children can do. These actions can be things like 'jump', 'hop', 'clap', 'star-jump', 'roar!', and anything else like that you can think of. It doesn't have to be too artistic – just a star shape for a star-jump for example.

Stand in a circle, and roll both dice. Then the children do whatever the dice tell them. It might be 'six star-jumps.' Go for it!

Great for one to one correspondence, and also for experiencing which numbers are larger than others. Children will really notice that six is bigger than one, for example, because they have to do so many more actions.

You can extend it in the following ways:

i) Use two number dice and add the two together

ii) Find one more of the number on the dice and do that quantity of actions

5. Dance Counting

Key Skills: One to one correspondence, rote counting, number recognition

This one is a beast!

Some source of music is important for this one, so if you can do that outside then great! Otherwise, it may be a safe bet to do inside.

Stand in a socially distanced circle, and put on some kind of pumping disco track. Pretty much anything with a good beat will work well.

Show them a number flashcard, for example '4'. Then you are going to teach them a simple dance routine, for example 'put your arms up four times, put them down four times, to the left, to the right.'

Then they are going to have a go. When they have done the routine, show them a different number, for example '2'. Do the same routine again, only with two of every number. Keep going like this with different numbers.

This is another good game for 'experiencing' the number. You start to understand how five is so much bigger than two because you have to dance for so much longer.

Later on, the children can invent their own moves, and this really adds to enthusiasm and engagement.

6. Count Round The Circle (In Different Ways)

Key Skills: Rote counting, counting on and back from given numbers, counting backwards, counting in 2s, 5s and 10s

This is an excellent game to practise counting in all sort of different ways.

You sit in a socially-distanced circle, and then the counting begins! The easiest way of doing it is to start at one. The teacher says 'one', the next child says 'two', the next 'three', and you just carry on like that around the circle.

This is much harder than just one individual counting from one, as we are programmed to count this way with lots of practice. In this game, it will just be a case of knowing what number comes next at any one point.

Other ways to do it are the following:

  i) Start at a random number, such as 6

  ii) Count backwards from 5, 10 or 20

  iii) Count in 2s, 5s or 10s

  iv) Count in silly voices

7.Counting An Instrument's Sounds

Key Skills: Counting sounds, one to one correspondence, representing numbers on fingers, counting in 2s, 5s and 10s

Counting sounds is a very different skill to counting objects, and this game is perfect for developing this.

The adult will have an instrument, and the children sit in a circle.

Quite simply, the adult hits the instrument a certain number of times and the children count. When you stop, they show how many hits you did on their fingers.

A similar game is dropping something noisy into a bucket. They find this strangely fascinating!

It is basically the same – you drop something like pebbles into a bucket and the children count.

Either this or the instrument game can be extended in the following ways:

i) Find one more or less of the quantity

ii) Each noise represents 10 or 2 (this will really get them thinking!). For example, if each noise was 10, then you count 10, 20, 30 for three pebble drops.

8. Puppet Counting

Key Skills: Rote counting, missing numbers, counting forwards and backwards

Puppets are like magic. They have a power to totally engage most children.

Use this to your advantage with some puppet maths.

Any puppet will work well for this. It could be a large puppet or just the finger variety. It could also be a doll or a teddy.

A good trick is for the puppet to always whisper. It whispers in your ear, and you tell the children what it has said. This seems to work far better than making up a pretend voice. The children then know it's you talking and this seems to break the magic somehow.

Anyway, some great counting games to play include:

i) The puppet counts and the children join in. Really simple!

ii) The puppet counts but then misses out a number. Children love to see incompetence in puppets (as well as adults!) They love being able to coach the puppet into how to do it right.

iii) The puppet counts backwards and they join in

iv) The puppet suggests a number to start counting from, and they all count forwards or backwards from that number

9.Numbers Numbers All Around

Key Skills: Number recognition, one to one correspondence, finding one more or less

This is possibly my favourite maths circle game for preschool, though it can be adapted later on as well.

Have some number flashcards that the adult will hold, and the children sit in a circle.

There is a song that goes with this game, that goes like this:

Numbers numbers all around!

Numbers numbers all around!

Numbers numbers all around!

What's the number you have found!

Any made up tune will be fine. I get them to do a bit of a dance for the song as well, which is quite hard to describe in written form. It basically involves lots of fist pumping!

Choose one child to go first. They stand up and you show them a number, e.g. 6. The child is going to jump and down slowly on the spot six times whilst everyone else claps and counts – '1, 2, 3, 4, 5, 6!'

Then someone else has a go. So simple and yet so multisensory. They really enjoy the clapping and jumping.

Ways to extend it are:

    i) Use more challenging numbers

    ii) Try different actions other than jumping

    iii) All children jump at the same time

    iv) Find one more or less of a number

10.Team Count

Key Skills: Rote counting in different ways

This is a bit like a maths tennis match.

You have two teams that face each other. Everyone in each team is sitting 2m apart.

Quite simply, one team is going to say 'one' and then the other team says 'two'. You keep going like that, bouncing forwards and backwards until it is clear they can go no further.

Ways to extend it include:

   i)   Count backwards
   ii) Count on from a given number
   iii) Count in 2s, 5s or 10s

11. Counting In Different Voices

Key Skills: Rote counting, counting backwards, counting on from a number, counting back from a number, counting in 2s, 5s and 10s.

This is quite simple really, but very good fun. It is excellent for engaging children that are not very interested in maths and counting. Also, without trying to be too sexist, it is a good one for boys, particularly if you count like dinosaurs or tigers or something similar.

Sit in some kind of socially distanced array, and then pick a voice to count like. Some good ones are:

    i)   A ghost

    ii) A zombie

    iii) Monster

    iv) Witch

    v) Princess

    vi) T-Rex

    vii)Tiger

    viii)   Alien

    ix) Robot

If the children are really interested in something I would use that to my advantage as well. If they love the Hulk, then count like the Hulk!

I have a dice with different characters drawn on that we roll, but this is not essential. Just mix it up.

Once again you can count in all the different ways – forwards, backwards, in 2s, 5s and 10s, and all the rest of it.

12. Action Counting

Key Skills: Rote counting

This is probably quite a well-known activity. You can do it to music, or you can just do it without.

You pick some kind of action, such as marching. You all start marching and count as you do it! Count for as far as you can until they clearly can't go any further.

Always count at least past ten, even with the very young ones. Some children think the numbers stop at ten, and that is not ideal. Go to eleven or twelve at the very least.

Then pick a different action, and start again from one.

This is good for beginning to think about odd and even numbers. For example, when you stamp your left leg it will be odd numbers, and the right will be even.

Doing actions that you do on one side then on the other are great to start building up a pattern of awareness that will later on grow into an understanding of odd and even numbers (with a bit of work!)

13. Estimate Flash

Key Skills: Estimating, counting, representing quantities on their fingers, subitising

This is a simple but effective estimating game.

The adult has a sheet and also some objects to go under it, for example pebbles. The idea is that the adult will put a quantity of pebbles under the sheet in such a way that the children are not able to count them whilst you do it.

Then you take the sheet off for only about a second before returning it over them. Give the children long enough to see objects, but not long enough to count.

The idea is that the children will then guess the quantity of objects by showing what they think on their fingers.

When they have all had a guess, show them and let them count.

Some children get very stressed if they have got it wrong, so that is in many ways a big focus of this activity. You don't need to get it right! Any sensible guess is 'right'. If there were 8 stones, then 0 would be a silly guess. But 6, 9, or 10 would all be fine.

14. Gathering Found Objects

Key Skills: One to one correspondence, shapes, matching numeral to quantity, and many more.

This last activity is a whole world of learning by itself.

Rooting around for found objects outside that only you are going to touch, is surely brilliant for social distancing.

Objects like sticks, stones, and leaves can be used in all sorts of mathematical learning experiences.

Some of these include:

i) Making shapes with sticks

ii) Matching a written numeral to a number of objects

iii) Making patterns, e.g. stick stone stick stone

iv) Adding two quantities – e.g. four orange leaves, add three red

CHAPTER 8

Circle Games

This book is brimming with many circle games that are perhaps more specific in the skills they develop, so I thought I should include a chapter of circle games that each contain a real mish-mash of features.

Circle games are a fantastic asset to social distancing, as you can control where people sit in a fun and structured way, that is not oppressive or over-bearing. It is just the way the game works.

These games are all great for:

    i) Cooperation

    ii) Teamwork

    iii) Eye contact

    iv) Turn-taking

    v) And many more interpersonal skills such as these

All these games are great played with children on rubber spots set out in a circle.

1. Pass the Expression

A reasonably simple game for children 3 upwards, that teaches them about eye contact, and also human emotion and how to spot it.

The adult goes first, and does some kind of facial expression towards the child that is sitting next to them. It could be a smile, a frown, a shocked face, or a sad face. Let's say we try a frown.

That child will frown to the person next to them, and they will pass it on to the next, and keep going all around the circle.

Then try a different type of facial expression. When they get the idea, a child can go first and decide the face that the others will copy.

2. Fruit Salad

This is a classic circle game that just needs a little tweak to adhere to social distancing. It might be an idea to put a circle of cones around the outside of where the children are sitting, setting it two metres away from the spots. This wider circle is where the children will run around the outside during the game.

Go around the circle telling each child which fruit they are. It is good to stick to about four different types of fruit, for example 'banana', 'apple', 'orange', and 'grape.'

The big thing is trying to get them to remember which fruit they are. If they can do that then happy times are here.

Then say a fruit, e.g. 'grape'. All the grapes stand up, turn round, and will run round the outside of the cones to find a spare place where one of the other grapes has stood up.

They will all find a new place (hopefully) and sit in it.

If you can get them all running the same direction, for example clockwise, then it will work even better.

3.Wake Up Giant Game

For this you have a similar set-up as for Fruit Salad, with a wide circle of cones around the outside of where the children are sitting.

One child will sit in the middle to start with. They are the giant. They close their eyes.

Pick one child to go first. They sneak up to near the giant (but not too near!)and shout 'Wake up, Giant!'

Then they turn around and run back to their place, but keep going and run once around the outer ring of cones, before running back through their place to the middle of the circle.

As soon as they have shouted, the giant is going to wake up and chase them! This will be a shadow tag situation again. The giant is going to try to stand on the child's shadow before they do the lap and back to the middle of the circle.

The child that was being chased then becomes the giant and repeat.

Top Tip – In reality the child's shadow will only be behind them for half the lap of the circle (and in front of them for the other half), so there is only a certain time when it is possible to 'strike'.

4.Swop Places

This is a much simpler version of Fruit Salad for younger children (probably those aged 3 and possibly 4).

Sit in a circle, and pick two children to go first. They stand up, turn around and run around the cones round the outside of the circle to go and sit in the other person's place. Simple as that!

Top Tip – I normally play this game (and fruit salad) as a parachute game where they run under the parachute, but I've adapted both for social distancing and no objects.

5.Blink Murder

This one is a real cracker-jack!

It is usually known as wink murder, but I find some children have real problems with winking with one eye, so it is definitely easier to play 'blink' murder, where two eyes are shutting at the same time.

The children sit in a circle, and one child is chosen to sit in the middle. They are the 'detective', and must first close their eyes.

Select one child to be the 'killer'. Probably the best way of doing this is by pointing to them silently.

Get the detective to open their eyes, and the game begins.

The idea is that the 'killer' will blink (or wink if they can) at different people in the circle. If the 'killer' winks at you then you 'die', and lie on the floor.

The 'killer' is trying not to get seen by the 'detective', and must try and blink when the 'detective' is looking elsewhere. The 'detective' is obviously trying to work out who the 'killer' is.

A really fun game, and one of the best that exist for practising eye contact.

6. Pass the Noise

This is a good one for eye contact, and also good for listening and communication skills.

Sit in a circle, and the adult makes a noise to the child next to them. The child copies this noise and passes it to the next child, and in this way the noise gets passed around the circle.

Good examples of noises to try out include:

i)   Animal noises, such as 'moo', 'roar', 'ssss' (like a snake)

ii) Sound effects, like 'bang', 'pop', or 'whizz'

iii) Character noises, such as a ghost ('woooo') or an evil cackling witch ('ha ha ha!')

iv) Phonics sounds, such as 't', 'p' or 'm'

7. Farmers in His Den

Circle songs are fantastic for structured outdoor play sessions.

Unfortunately, lots do include holding hands or other types of contact, but some can definitely be adapted to suit social distancing.

Here is a good example of this – The Farmer's In His Den.

To begin the game, have some rubber spots dotted around the centre of the circle, each two metres away from the other circles.

Stand in a socially distanced circle, and pick one child to come and stand in the centre of the circle on one of the spots. This is the farmer.

Then all sing:

The farmer's in the den

The farmer's in the den

Ee I addio,

The farmer's in the den.

Then for the next verse, the farmer is going to pick a wife, so before that happens you sing:

The farmer wants a wife,

The farmer wants a wife (etc)…

The farmer picks someone to be the wife, and that person comes and stands on another spot.

In the next verse:

The wife wants a child...

Out comes a child to stand on a spot.

Keep going like this. The other verses are:

The child wants a nurse...

The nurse wants a dog...

The dog wants a bone...

In the old days you would finish with 'we all pat the bone' but I would just leave that out now.

There are probably lots of other circle songs that you can adapt in a similar way to this.

8. Pass The Blink

This is another simple passing game, good for eye contact and teamwork.

The adult blinks to the first child in the circle, who passes the blink to the child next to them, and so on around the circle.

If they can wink then do that – certainly children of six years plus can have a go of winking (and possibly a few younger ones as well).

9. Pass the Rhythm

This is a great phonics circle game of which there are quite a few versions.

To start with the easiest version, sit in a circle, and the adult says a word, and claps the syllables as they are saying it.

For example, they might go 'mo-tor-bike' whilst clapping the three syllables.

Then the child next to you goes 'motorbike' and claps. Then the next person goes. Pass it round the circle like this.

Another way of doing this is just as a call and answer game. The adult says a word, and all the children copy.

Another version that is just slightly harder, is one at a time the children say a word and clap the syllables. Then everyone in the circle copies, before you go on to the next child.

It is good to pick a theme if you do this. It could be favourite foods, or their names.

A much harder version of the game is where you use no word but just clap a rhythm, and the children try to copy it. Different ways of doing this include:

> i) Call and answer. Clap a rhythm and the children copy
>
> ii) Clap a rhythm and pass it round the circle.
>
> iii) One at a time a child does a rhythm and everyone copies

These games are fantastic for listening, eye contact, and auditory sequential memory.

10.Duck Duck Goose (Adapted)

This is a really classic outdoor game, adapted only slightly with social distancing in mind.

Sit in a wide circle, and have an inner circle of spots that is two metres inside the outer circle.

One child is 'it'. They walk round the inner circle of spots pointing at one child in turn and saying 'duck, duck, duck…' Eventually they will point at a child and say 'goose.' The goose is going to chase them!

It's one lap round the inner circle of spots and back to where the child was sitting. It's another shadow tag situation, so this game needs to be done outside in this format. The goose tries to stand on the other child's shadow.

11.Zoom Zoom Zoom Song

This is a simple counting backwards game, and probably my favourite song for teaching this skill.

Stand in a circle, and have socially-distanced spots dotted around the middle of the space as well.

The adult walks round the inner part of the circle, pointing at each child in turn and going '10,9,8,7…' It is one number for one point at a child. The children join in. The child that is 'zero' is chosen to be an astronaut. They come and stand on one of the spots in the middle.

Then do the same process again, counting back from 10 and finally selecting an astronaut. Pick about 4 or 5 astronauts, then you are ready for the big launch.

Get everyone to put on imaginary space-boots, suits and helmets. This is whether they are in the circle or in the middle – everyone is going to the moon! Then sing the song:

Zoom zoom zoom

We're going to the moon

Zoom zoom zoom

We'll be there very soon

10, 9, 8, 7, 6, 5, 4, 3, 2, 1, 0. Blast off!

Pretend to blast off and fly to the moon (whilst all standing on the spot).

12. Act The Emotion

This is another good game for eye contact and understanding human emotion and how to spot it in others.

Have three pictures, one of a happy face, one of a sad, and one of an angry. Put these in the middle of the circle.

One at a time a child is going to stand up and walk around the circle, pretending to show one of these emotions. For example, if you are happy you will have a joyful face and head held high, and be skipping or walking briskly. For miserable, on the other hand, you might walk with hunched shoulders, unhappy face, and slow steps.

The other children are going to try to guess which emotion you are showing.

You can all talk about features you can spot, such as facial expressions and body language.

CHAPTER 9

Physical Games

This is a chapter of physical games that might be great as a PE session, or for use during other more structured outdoor sessions.

Lots combine multiple skills – listening, imagination, memory, and a range of gross motor skills.

There are pretty much no resources required for any of them, with the exception of a few rubber spots as markings on the ground, and the odd instrument for an adult.

1.Rabbit Game

This is a highly addictive game that many children will love.

You will need at least one instrument, and three different instruments if you are going to do the harder version of the game.

Put out lots of rubber spots in a random array all over the floor. The spots should all be at least two metres apart, and you need at least as many spots as children. The spots are the rabbit holes.

The children are now the rabbits. They are going to hop around the 'field' (which is the playing area).

Have an instrument such as a drum. This is the 'fox'. When the children hear the fox, they will need to get to a rabbit quick and stand on it. Then they are safe.

Repeat the game, getting them to move in different ways – for example, hopping, skipping, crawling, jumping sideways etc.

There are a few ways you can expand the game. These include:

Adding more instruments and animals. When you shake the tambourine, that is the friendly snake. The children will just carry on. A maraca is the monkey. He's your friend, so when you hear that you're going to wave. The drum is still the fox, and that still means hide.

Another way of playing is the competitive version. In this, the fox comes back each time and takes away a few holes. Then when they hear the drum next time some children will be 'out'. They go and sit somewhere in a socially distanced way.

At the end one child (or a group of children) will be the champion/s.

2.Captain's Coming

This is a fun role-playing game, that combines physical activity with imagination.

The children are all sailors on the boat. There are different commands that you demonstrate to them, and actions they will do when they hear each one. These are:

Captain's coming – Stand on the spot and salute

Row the boat – Sit down and row

Scrub the deck – Down on your knees and scrub

Swim to shore – Swim!

Into the hammock – Lie down

Lift the cannonballs – Lift them up one by one and put them in the cannon

Just mix up the commands and let them go for it.

3.Funny Races

The idea of this one is to move like different animals in a race.

Have some kind of starting line, with the children socially distanced. Then pick the type of animal you are going to try. Either the adult can suggest the idea, or the children can make it up themselves.

It is good to have a demonstration from someone on how to move like that animal first.

Some good animals are things like:

    i) Monkeys

    ii) Horses

    iii) Chickens

    iv) Snakes

    v) Eagles

    vi) A T-rex

Ideally this is best done on grass, as you might have a few monkeys tripping over.

4.Traffic Lights

This is a great listening game that involves all sorts of gross motor skills.

The children are the cars in this game. The adult is going to be the traffic light.

The instructions the traffic light will give, and the actions the children do, are the following:

Green – Go! Jog around the space

Red – Stop

Amber – Walk on the spot, waiting

Start off like this. You can either say the instructions verbally, or a slightly harder version is you have three markers – one green, one red and one amber. You hold these up now and again.

This encourages the children to always be alert and on the lookout for the next signal.

You can extend this game with the following ideas:

Car-park – They lie down

Motorway (or freeway) – Run really fast

Honk the horn – Beep! Beep!

Roundabout – Go round in a circle

5.Zombie Race

This is a fun race to use towards the end of a session as a bit of good old-fashioned enjoyment.

The idea of this is that it is a race with the one rule being that you can't bend your legs. The children will basically look at bit like zombies as they give it a try.

6.Bean Game

This is another quite well-known listening game.

The children are going to move around like different beans. The instructions the adult will give in this game, and the corresponding actions are these:

Runner bean – the children run around

Sprouting bean – walk on tip-toes, with arms high in the air

Jelly bean – wobble like jelly

Baked bean – sit down

Beans on toast – lie down

Chilli bean – shiver!

Broad bean – Put your arms out as wide as possible

French bean – Say 'Bonjour!

I would say to start simple with this – maybe show them about three or four different types of beans to begin with, and expand as they get used to them.

You can extend the game by getting a child to become the person giving instructions.

7.Simon Says

Another old chestnut from the repertoire here – Simon Says.

This probably needs no real introduction, but just for the record...

The adult gives an instruction by first saying 'Simon says…'
So it could be 'Simon says, "Put your hands on your head".'
The children do it. 'Simon says, "Jump three times".'

If you miss out the 'Simon says' and just say the instruction, then the idea is that the children do not do it. For example, if you say 'Hop on the spot,' they shouldn't do it.

8.Mr Men Or Little Miss Game

This is a very simple concept, and one that is open to lots of creativity and suggestions from children.

The idea is that you are all going to move around the space like different Mr Men or Little Miss characters.

Some good suggestions might be:

Mr Grumpy – Stamp round with angry faces

Mr Tall – Walk as high as possible with arms up

Mr Topsy-Turvy – Walk, jump or crawl backwards

Little Miss Tiny – Move round in a curled-up ball

Little Miss Sunshine – Skip joyfully around

If children can suggest their own characters and movements then that is great. I have only skimmed the surface here of the all the possible Mr Men and Little Miss characters that you could try.

This game could also be adapted to a more general idea of different characters from stories. They could move like the Gruffalo, or the Big Bad Wolf for example.

9.Different Races

Races are good for maintaining social distancing simply, and there are many ways you can try different kinds of race.

One way is to try to move in many different ways. You could try some of the following:

i)   A jumping race

ii) Hopping

iii) Skipping

iv) Jumping sideways

v) Speed walking

Very simple but enjoyable. If you arrange where children sit at the start and end in socially distanced lines, you can have small groups racing against each other one at a time, or you could just do it with a larger group of children all at once.

10. Freeze

This is a simple and fun warm-down game.

The children stand on socially-distanced spots and all do a freestyle dance. Then the adult says 'Freeze!' You could use a magic wand for added mystical excitement, but this is completely optional!

The children are going to try to freeze! You walk around, and if anyone is moving they are eliminated and will lie down on the floor.

You could have a child or several children walking round and picking who is moving.

You can do it in a way that there is a champion at the end, or just that at the conclusion everyone will be lying on the floor and cooling down after everything you have done.

CHAPTER 10

Relay Games

Here are some fun outdoor games that are a mixture of relay races and listening and attention games.

All these require no equipment. It is hard to do traditional relay races within strict social distancing, as these require passing things between team members, or tagging each other's hands. Therefore, I have had to be a bit creative.

For all of these races, split however many children you have into teams. They will sit in straight lines, each child 2 metres apart from the others. Your teams would line up side-by-side, again following the two metre distance guideline.

Here we go:

1. Race on the Spot

The idea of this is to pick some kind of movement that every child will do on the spot. A good example would be ten jumps.

The first children in each team stand up. After 'Ready, steady, go!' they each do ten jumps on their spot. When they have finished they sit, and the next person in their line stands up and does the same.

The winning team are those that are all finished and sat down first. Someone might have to go twice if there are uneven team numbers.

This could be extended by having a sequence of movements. The first leg could be ten jumps. Then back to the beginning for five star jumps, and carry on like this. Have three or four legs.

2. Mexican Wave Relay

This seems quite simple, but young children take a while to get the hang of this skill.

Basically you will pass a 'Mexican Wave' down the line and back again. You could do this several times, for example seeing which is the first team to do five waves up and down the line.

This could also be done in a non-competitive way with just one long line of children all in one team.

3. Back-To-Back Relay

This is probably as close to a traditional relay as you can get (in strict social distancing).

Two teams are required for this, and you line up next to each other in two long lines. The two teams are going to be sat so that their backs are turned to each other.

About twenty metres in front of one team put one cone, and over on the other side put a similar cone about twenty metres in front of the other team.

The idea is that the first person at the end of the line will start. On the command of 'ready, steady, go', they will run round the cone and back to their space. Then the next person in the line will go, round the cone and back.

Keep going until everyone has gone, and the team all sitting down first are the winners.

4.Counting Race

This is good for one whole team, but you could do it as a race as well if you preferred.

The basic idea of this is that the first person in the line is going to say '1', the next person '2' and continue like this up and down the line. You could have a target number that you are trying to get to, for example, twenty.

CHAPTER 11

Early Phonics and Literacy Games

The following games have all grown out of phase one phonics activities, but that definitely does not mean they are just for very young children. The skills involved in these games can be used across the ages to develop key skills such as alliteration, rhyme and general listening. They can be used for poetry, or for teaching phonemes.

Once again, very little equipment is required. Just enthusiasm and energy to make it work.

1.Alliteration Dance

This is a brilliant game to teach alliteration, but you can use it to teach letters and sounds also.

Put some pumping music on, preferably some kind of disco track without any words.

Then pick a sound, for example 's'. The idea is that you are all going to chant words that begin with that sound to the music!

I would chant it at least four times per word. For example, 'Slide, slide, slide, slide.' As you do the word, it is good to bring it to life with an action as well. Just make these up! For example, whizz your hand down through the air for a slide.

Get them all joining in, and then try different words. Good examples could be 'snake…snow…swim…sneeze…'

If the children can come up with their own words then that is brilliant and exactly what you want. If not, then just come up with your own.

You can use this game to teach phonemes by showing them a flashcard, e.g. an 's', and then doing the same game.

2. Copy the Sequence

Sit in a socially distanced circle for this one.

The adult is going to do a simple sequence by patting different parts of their body. You will do three pats.

For example, it could be 'head, knees, feet.' The children try to copy. Do it nice and slow to start with to give them a good chance of doing it well, and also repeat each sequence a few times.

The harder version is that one at a time a child will make up a sequence and the others try to copy it.

The big rule, to comply with social distancing, is not to touch your face.

Great for eye contact, memory, and listening and attention in particular.

3. Story Sound Effects

This is a cocktail of early phonics and storytelling.

The idea of this is that the adult makes up some kind of a story. The children are going to provide sound effects in the story by clapping their hands, banging the floor, patting their legs – anything that will create some kind of sound that will match the story.

Some great features to include are things like:

i) Bad character stamping, smashing things down, or roaring

ii) Little characters scuttling, flying or dancing

iii) The noises of animals moving – horses, unicorns, snakes

iv) Object noises, like squeaky doors

v) Animal noises

vi) People moving – running, swimming, flying

If the children can get involved in inventing the story then that is great. If they can completely take over then even better!

If not, just tell it yourself and see how it goes.

An example of a start might something like 'One day the terrible dragon woke up in it's cave. It stamped across the cave – *stamp, stamp, stamp*. It roared a terrible roar – *ROAR!'*

Encourage them to make the sound effects with their mouths, clap their hands, and hit their legs and the floor and anything else.

4. Cross the River

This is one of the all-time great early phonics games that is usually played with objects.

However, here we are going to give it a try without any resources that the children will hold.

Sit in a circle, and have some kind of pretend river in the middle. This could be something like a blue sheet, or a couple of lines drawn on the ground with chalk.

Pick about three children to go at a time. They will stand on one bank of the river, each spaced out two metres from the others.

There is a song that everyone sings. It goes to the music of 'She'll be coming round the mountain when she comes,' and the words are:

You'll be crossing the river when it's you!

You'll be crossing the river when it's you!

You'll be crossing the river, crossing the river,

Crossing the river when it's you!

Now you are going to give a clue of which child should cross the river first. Some ways of doing it could be:

i) Initial sound of their name, such as 'Whose name begins with 't'.'

ii) A rhyming version of their name – such as 'I know someone called Warlie, Cross over the river....' (Charlie will cross)

5. Rhythm Bag Clap

There are many different ways you can do this, but the basic idea is to get some kind of a feely bag and put a few different objects into it.

It is good if you pick some kind of a theme, such as superheroes or food, for example. I am going to give an example of jungle animals.

Put about three or four toy animals into the bag. Try to use animals that have a different number of syllables in their names, for example:

Snake – one syllable

Tiger – two

Crocodile – three

Now you all say a chant or a song that links to the theme, whilst clapping the beat.

For example, for the jungle animals you can use this song:

Walking through the jungle,

Walking through the jungle,

What do I see? What do I see?

Then take out an animal, e.g. the tiger. The idea is to clap the word 'tiger', and then count the syllables. So you go 'ti (clap)-ger (clap). 1 (clap), 2 (clap)!' Clap at the same time as you say the syllable.

Repeat what you have said a few times, so everyone gets the hang of it. Then get another animal out of the bag.

Top Tip – If the children are really interested in something then I would use that. For example, if they loved dinosaurs, then put some of them in a bag and try that game out.

6. Clap The Sentence

This is a slightly trickier version of the last game. Instead of words, now we are clapping whole sentences.

Sit in a socially distanced circle for this one.

This is great for children aged 3-5 to try, to learn how to split up sentences orally, but it is also beneficial for older children who are working on sentence writing.

Give them a simple sentence, such as 'brush your teeth.' Everyone says it and claps the words, and then counts as well – 'Brush your teeth! 1-2-3!'

Try with different phrases, such as 'Go on the bus! 1-2-3-4!'

You can also use silly voices. Try saying it like aliens, or dinosaurs, or ghosts.

Older children can attempt to write the sentence also. The clapping process first helps the sentence stick in their minds, and supports their understanding of how a sentence is broken up into words.

7.Sound Story

This is an excellent game for practising alliteration, and also can be used to teach phonemes as well.

In general, I think there is a strong connection between most alliteration games and teaching sounds.

For this game, pick a sound that is going to feature a lot in a story that you are going to make up. For example, it might be a story with lots of 't' sounds in it.

Tell the children that if they hear a 't' in the story they are going to do an action. It could be pat their knees, or maybe do the phonic action for the sound.

Then make up a story. It could be something like, 'One day *Tom* went out of his house. He was a *turtle*. He went down the road where he saw a *tiger*.'

Really emphasise the 't' sounds when they come up so that the children can hear them. If you are teaching phonemes through this method, show them what the letter looks like first, and also show them the action if you are using one. They can practise this as they listen for the sound in the story.

8. Action Segmenting

Segmenting is definitely a skill that should be made as physical and active as possible. The more multisensory you make it, the quicker the children grasp the concept.

Segmenting is simply splitting words up into their phonemes (sounds). It is a key skill of early writing in particular. For example, you split the word 'dog' up like this - 'd-o-g.'

One simple way to practise is by moving and segmenting at the same time. Here are some great ideas to try:

i)   Jump and segment! E.g. use three jumps and go 's-i-t.' Then one final jump for the whole word – 'sit!'

ii) Clap

iii) March

iv) Dance!

9. Freeze Frame

This is a game that works well with children from about the age of five upwards.

It is excellent for thinking more deeply about how characters are feeling in stories, and it merges reading a story with drama.

Sit the children in a socially distanced circle, and show them a page of a book that they already know well. It ideally will be a picture of something really exciting in the book – a key moment. How will the character respond?

Get them all on their feet, and then they are going to act out how they think the character will react!

As an example, it could be the Big Bad Wolf as he falls down the chimney and sees he is about to land in a pot of boiling water.

They act like the wolf might, and then 'Freeze!' Tell them to freeze exactly as they are.

Then you go round and ask them questions. It could be things like 'Why is your mouth open?' 'How are you feeling?' 'What do you think is about to happen?' 'Why are your arms like this?'

Any questions that generate talk and engagement with that point in the story.

10.One Sentence Story

This is a slightly more challenging game, probably for children from 5 upwards.

It is a beautiful storytelling experience when it works well, requiring no resources.

Sit the children in a socially-distanced circle. The adult starts a story off with a single sentence. It could be something like 'One day a unicorn went into the forest.'

Then the next child will carry on the story by saying a sentence, e.g. 'It saw a monster.'

Carry on round the circle, with each child offering roughly one sentence at a time to keep the story going.

Don't worry if they do two or more sentences. Keeping them to one sentence can be challenging when they are on a creative roll.

Also, don't be concerned about the story ever coming to a natural or logical conclusion. Just keep going and the more random the better.

Final Thoughts

Although I have a new-found dread of the word 'unprecedented', having heard it far too much recently, that is the perfect description of the times we are in as educators – unprecedented.

We will just have to give it a go and make the most of the knowledge, skills and common sense that we possess. There will so much to be learned at the coal-face.

Hopefully, however, the games in this book will be part of your armoury in tackling the many challenges that we will experience.

If you're looking for a mini version of these games, I have condensed them all into one bite-sized single cheat sheet. You can download this for free from this link – www.earlyimpactlearning.com/cheat

Good luck with these games, and best wishes over the times ahead!

The End

Printed in Great Britain
by Amazon